KEEPING THE LIGHT ON

Faith & Prayers
for the Spiritual Awakening of Loved Ones

DON WILKERSON

Table of Contents

Introduction...5

1. The Power of Light..9

2. A Lamb for a Household....................................12

3. Nan's Homecoming and Home Going...................17

4. Jerry!..21

5. Jerry's Homecoming.......................................26

6. Walking and Praying in the Light......................32

7. The Olive Tree Promise..................................38

8. Mothers and Other Who Kept the Light On............45

9. The Most Difficult Question............................54

10. Grandparents Who Keep the Light On.................63

11. The Lamp Lighters.......................................70

About the Author..73
Recommended Reading List..................................74

Introduction

In Him was life, and the life was the light of men.
And the light shines in the darkness...
(John 1:4-5)

The inspiration for *Keeping The Light On* is from the picture that comes to my mind whenever I read, teach, or preach from the Parable of the Prodigal Son. The image that stands out to me is that of the father every evening sitting on the front porch, looking down a long pathway from his vantage point. He's watching, waiting, praying, and wondering—might this be the night of my wayward son's return? In hopes of the prodigal's return, there's a lamp just inside the house whose light can be seen from a far distance.

When the father retires for the night, he makes sure that lamp in the window is filled with oil so that it's light will be seen if his son returns in the darkness of night. The light in the window is to help his lost son find his way home. Night after night that light shines both as a sign of welcome and as a reflection of the light of hope in the father's heart as he continues to pray for his wayward son's homecoming.

Then one evening—in my imagination, it's around sunset—the father sees someone just outside the property gate. Is it, could it be, the son he has hoped and prayed to return! As the figure draws closer, he suddenly realizes, yes, it is his long-lost son. He jumps up and runs, runs to embrace him. Finally, the lost one has been found! Soon the full meaning and drama of the Parable of the Prodigal unfolds as recorded in Luke, Chapter 15. The story gives faith and hope to every father, mother, and family members of runaway prodigals whose mission is to pray for their loved one's return to his or her home and family.

Some years ago, I heard a commercial on the radio numerous times for a motel chain that had the tag line, "We'll leave the light on for you." The meaning was that even if someone needed a room in the darkness of night *leaving the light on* was an invitation that a room would always and surely be available to whomever needed one, whenever they needed it. Every time I heard that commercial, I'd envision the prodigal son's father leaving the light on as an invitation and welcome for his son to come home, even in the dark of night.

Lights left on at night signify that there is life inside. Light in the spiritual realm and in the *super*-natural is also a sign of life, faith, and hope inside the heart of the one praying, waiting, keeping faith alive for the day their prodigal will return. If you are praying for a prodigal, "leaving the light on" can have several meanings which we will explore. So let the Light of Christ always be perpetually lit in the hopes of your prodigal returning home and returning to Christ. This happened in my own family, the Wilkerson household. I witnessed both my oldest sister and one of my brothers experience a wonderful return after a long season of wandering away from God. My sister was a successful Special Education teacher. My brother, for many years, was a grocery store manager who slowly descended into alcoholism. Much like the prodigal son in the parable, both came to the Lord after years of prayers by our family. I hope you will be inspired by their stores in the upcoming chapters.

I write this to everyone who is or has been like the prodigal's father—waiting, agonizing, praying for a glorious homecoming. Are you one of the waiting ones? Are you crying for your prodigal, begging God to lead them back home, and yet, your loved one just grows worse and worse? Maybe you're tempted to blame God. Maybe you blame yourself, if only you had known God sooner. Perhaps, as a believer, you wonder what you may have done wrong. I am writing to you! I have some "Light" to shed on your struggles.

1

The Power of Light

The light shines in the darkness, and the darkness can never extinguish it (John 1:5 NLT).

I've worked with troubled youth and addicted prodigals of all ages for decades, and I can tell you that I have seen miracle after miracle of changed lives. I've witnessed their loved ones leaving the light of faith, hope, and prayer on as they believed that their prodigal would someday return home to the family and to Father God. I have been blessed so many times to see their "someday" become "today" as their son, daughter, mother or father found salvation and lasting deliverance. I'm not just writing about addicted loved one having a spiritual awakening, but about all those who have strayed from family and God for whatever reason, and yet, their loved ones persevered in prayer for them.

This book, *Keeping the Light On*, is my prophetic word to every parent, spouse, grandparent, sibling, and loved one who has kept the light in their heart on for their loved one gone astray from their faith and their family. In some cases, the light has grown dim as the heart has grown weary in well doing over time. The expectation of the prodigal's return can seem more and more improbable as time goes by.

For others, the light is just a flicker and soon all hope and faith for the prodigal's return is about to go dark. If this is the case, then this is a call to relight the flame of faith, hope, and prayer for a miracle, such as depicted in the famous Parable of Jesus.

Here's what God's message is to you:

1. **Jesus is "the Light of the world"** (John 8:12). As long as He lives as the Light in your heart and your home, through your prayers to God your loved one's return is possible.

2. God's Word is a Light shining the truth that it is His desire to see your loved one have a spiritual awakening. **"Your word is a lamp to my feet and a light to my path"** (Psalm 119:105). Christ is the Light who will lead your loved one on the pathway to God.

3. The Light of Christ shines on all—the lost as well as the found—to show the way home. **"That was the true Light which gives light to every man coming into the world"** (John 1:9).

4. Your loved one may reject the Light, but it still will always shine the way straight to the cross. Romans 2:19 says, God is **"a guide to the blind, a light to those who are in darkness."**

5. Be like Paul, who wrote to the church in Rome **"that without ceasing I make mention of you always in my prayers"** (Romans 1:9).

Exodus 10:23 says during the three-day plague of darkness in Egypt that "...all the children of Israel had light in their dwellings." God's Light is overshadowing your loved one even though it may be hidden to them because they are living in their own darkness. If your loved one did not know the Light of truth in Christ or the Light of God's Word in your home, God's light often shines on them in other ways, such as through the light of reason, conscience, and in nature, the beautiful creation by which they are surrounded. In addition, twice yearly, there is the celebration of Christmas and Easter which are opportunities for the Light of Truth to lead them to the Savior. You'd be surprised how the Holy Spirit reveals the Light of truth to those in darkness. The more unsaved loved ones are lifted up in prayer, the more the Light of Christ is revealed to them in different ways and through various signs, particularly if they have a desire to find such signs. That Light desires to be expressed in your hearts through the light of prayer.

I write for and dedicate this book to you who have (or want to develop) the Light of faith and prayers in your heart, as I imagine the father of the prodigal did. This I do know, God wants all of you and yours to have a spiritual awakening. He wants the Light of Christ to shine in the hearts and lives of your dear, wandering prodigals. Do your part in prayer and God will certainly do His.

2

A Lamb for a Household

Every man shall take for himself a lamb, according to the house of his father, a lamb for a household (Exodus 12:3).

I grew up in a minister's home where we believed that this verse from Exodus spoke of the promise of Jesus coming as "the lamb of God that takes away the sin of the world." It is a promise that everyone can experience—the forgiveness of our sins and a new life in Christ. When the death angel was about to enter Egypt and take the firstborn child of every family, the Lord provided a means by which every Israelite's home and child would be saved:

> Now the blood [on the door post of each Israelite household] shall be a sign for you on the houses where you are. And when I see the blood, I will pass over you; and the plague shall not be on you to destroy you when I strike the land of Egypt (Exodus 12:13).

But what happens when one or more people in a household do not claim that promise? It does not change the fact of the promise. Our parents in the Wilkerson household claimed this promise for my two prodigal siblings. It was one of the greatest challenges to our faith and prayers as a family to claim this for my oldest sister, Juanita and my brother

Jerry. Part of the challenge included guilt. I'll share the guilt part later, but for now I share encouragement if you or your family has had a Juanita who went astray. In my sister Juanita's case, she was very successful as a Special Education teacher married to a businessman and they raised two successful sons. But she was not living as a daughter of God. But for her continual prayers were made by my mother and her siblings, including myself, that someday this wayward daughter would find her way home to Father God.

Misguided Light

Nan, as I called her, was ten years older than me. Because I could not at first pronounce her given name, Juanita, she became Nan to me, and it stuck all throughout our lives. Juanita's straying from the faith of our father and mother began early. As she grew older and more rebellious, we siblings came to understand the root of her departure from the faith. As the firstborn into a strict Pentecostal holiness household, it meant Nan was subjected to being smothered by legalism. Our parents defined the world outside of the confines of our faith as worldly. This applied to wearing the latest fashion, going to theaters, watching TV, and participating in sports. Many other things were labeled sin by our church and parents, although they were not so labeled in the Bible. For example, the verse in the King James Version that says, "Bodily exercise profiteth little" (1 Timothy 4:8), my parents took to the extreme having been sadly influenced by the legalism in their church that did not allow any participation in sports activities.

By the time I came into the household, our parents had lightened up, but it was too late for Juanita. She saw Christianity as a straitjacket and went her own way even though she did attend Bible College for a year. According to my other sister Ruth, Juanita did have a true experience with the Lord before she went her own way. Proverbs 4:23 says, "Guard your heart above all else, for it determines the course of your life." Nan did not! So, my mother, like the father of the prodigal son, kept the light on always for her return.

Nan and mom were at odds most of their lives, especially when she embraced a New Age philosophy and took many opportunities to sound off about how she was raised. Mother did not know how to handle Juanita and finally found the best way to deal with her daughter was to lift her up in prayer. For more than fifty years mother kept the light on, keeping faith in her heart that her firstborn prodigal daughter would one day come home to the Light.

Out of all the family, I had the best relationship with my oldest sister mainly because of our age difference and because I never said anything negative to her. I find often in dealing with prodigals a sibling can be in a better position to relate to them—although that certainly did not happen in the biblical Parable of the Prodigal Son and his angry older brother. I was the only one in the family invited to spend time with her in the places she lived. At such times, we were just sister and brother, avoiding family talk and the past, and religious topics. Once, when eating at a restaurant, she did talk about writing a book. (I'm sure it would have been along the line of "Mommy Dearest" a negative exposé of her upbringing.) I simply said to her, "Nan, maybe a better way to deal with the past is to see a therapist." She grew silent! I'm sure this surprised her coming from her normally supportive little brother. The fact that I, a preacher, would recommend therapy probably also surprised her. Nan gave me a long look and then changed the subject.

We rarely had family discussions about Juanita, especially regarding her departure from the faith. Sadly, I do not recall her being lifted up before the Lord in our family prayer times, but I'm sure we did. I think the reason for this is that our parents carried guilt over their part in causing Nan to go off the straight and narrow. I've found in my ministry experience that guilt over a prodigal expresses itself in different ways: remembering or trying to forget (or denying) the spiritual and moral shortcomings in the way a child was raised. In praying for prodigals, it is important to ask God for forgiveness if there was hurt produced in the household. Once that is done the best thing parents, grandparents, siblings, and other believing family members can do is claim the principal and promise of "a lamb for a house."

Juanita was raised in our strict Pentecostal holiness household, so when she entered high school, she was required to abide by strict clothing rules and other harsh restrictions. That laid the roots of what would later feed her bitterness towards God, the church, and especially her mother. Nevertheless, at the time, she complied. She even took steps to follow the call of God into ministry and attended a Bible College...for one year. After that, she took the path of a prodigal, ended up, not in a dirty pigpen, but with some moderate success in life including a good husband.

I rarely saw her over the years, but when I did, I was aware of the light of faith staying on for her by our family, especially my mother, as she continued to believe for her recommitment to Christ. Juanita did have a glorious homecoming as did the prodigal son. Lest there be any misunderstanding, let me say that "a lamb for a house" principal does not imply that children are automatically saved through the faith of their saved parents. I believe they are preserved unto salvation, however. That is, the faith of the parents protects the children both as children and adult children from the Destroyer until they make their own personal commitment, or recommitment, to Christ. 1 Corinthians 7:14 in the Message Bible says:

> The unbelieving husband shares to an extent in the holiness of his wife, and the unbelieving wife is likewise touched by the holiness of her husband. Otherwise, your children would be left out; as it is, they also are included in the spiritual purposes of God.

Even when a loved one is far from God in faith or practice, the "lamb for a house" promise can be claimed by faith. Prodigals are still biologically, emotionally, and spiritually one with their family. Just ask any parent who has experienced either a physical or spiritual distance separation from their adult child. Praying parents and loved ones can continue to renew their faith and prayers and ask for the Spirit of God through the blood of Jesus to cover those not yet enjoying the blessings of salvation. I know our family did, for my sister Juanita for a long period of time (and anguish).

3

Nan's Homecoming and Home Going

As for me, I will come into Your house in the multitude of mercies; in fear of You I will worship towards Your holy temple (Psalm 5:7).

Prayers for a loved one can test the faith of those praying for them like nothing else. I find when the prodigal has grown up in the church, as in my sister's case, that challenge is compounded. Waiting in faith and in prayers can test the most dedicated prayer warrior. I would go weeks, even months, forgetting to pray for Nan. Our mother would not. She prayed daily for over fifty years for Nan's spiritual awakening. Yet, as I will show in detail, of all the ironic parts of this miracle, I was the one to witness it. The wait was worth it for me when I finally, at her dying bedside, was able to lead Nan in prayer back to her Savior. I experience, in the blinking of an eye, her homecoming to Jesus followed soon after by her home-going to heaven.

In the Old Testament, the Israelites had a daily reminder of the blood's purpose. Every time they entered the door of their house the stain was there to see. May we be reminded every day that our house is also under the blood, and renew our faith, our prayers, and our claim to its power. When it came to my sister Nan, the Wilkerson family's waiting finally came to an end. It happened when I ended up at Nan's bedside in a hospital in Tempe, Arizona some weeks after her son had called to say she had cancer. It was moving fast through her body. I told him, "If her condition gets worse, please call me." He did a few weeks after saying, "If you want to see your sister, you'd better come soon." I immediately booked a flight. When I got to the hospital, to my surprise the daughter-in-law of my sister's son was reading the Bible to her. It truly was a "surprise" because I knew the son and his wife were far from being believers.

A nurse was just leaving the room. When I came in, she said to me, "Go ahead and talk to her. She will understand you, but she won't verbally respond." I went to Nan's bedside and said, "Nan, it's your brother Don." She immediately blinked her eyes. I realized that was her only means of communication. After some minutes of pause and having said some brief words that I cannot recall, I said, "Nan, I want to pray for you." She blinked her eyes again, telling me she understood and agreed to let me do so. At that point the daughter-in-law graciously left the room. What took place then, to this day, sends chills up my arm.

Homecoming

I then said, "Nan, are you ready to meet God?" She did not respond. I said, "I'm going to pray the sinner's prayer for you to receive the Lord in your heart, if you have not already done so." I prayed a simple prayer and said, "Nan, do you agree with me in that prayer?" She immediately gave me a strong double wink. And in that moment, all the years of Juanita's turning away from the Lord, her rebellion, agnosticism, and sin was washed away by the blood of the Lamb.

She had once visited our church in Manhattan (Times Square Church). As we left the service, my daughter Julie was with us and asked Juanita, "How did you like the service?" She sarcastically answered with the words: "Nice show."

All those years of having lived a somewhat successful life (but rebelliously without God) were changed in a twinkling of an eye. Juanita was instantly healed of her cancer, for death is the ultimate healing, and in a few more hours she would be ushered into the presence of God in heaven. God favored me in being the one to lead my sister Nan in a deathbed repentance. Later that night her husband asked if I'd sleep in their bed as he could not bring himself to do so. I obliged. I noted that on a small table next to their bed was a Bible. Apparently, Nan had been reading that Bible, and I knew God had used her cancer trial to draw her back to Himself. There was a bookmark in the Bible. It was Ecclesiastics 8:12 from *The Message Bible*:

> Even though a person sins and gets by with it hundreds of times throughout a long life, I'm still convinced the good life is reserved for the person who fears God, who lives reverently in his presence.

The next day I preached at Juanita's funeral and used that as my text! Praise the Lord! My sister Ruth told me that about a month before her passing, she found out Juanita was trying to come to terms with the meaning of "the fear of the Lord." Apparently, she was living in the fear of meeting God. Ruth explained that when the Bible speaks about "the fear of the Lord" it means reverence for Him. "I never knew that" Juanita had humbly responded. From this and from seeing the verse from Ecclesiastes, I realized Nan had sorted out her relationship to God and was ready to meet Him. However, it was good, especially for mine and my family's sake, to have those few moments to pray for her and with her in the hospital. I likened it to a deathbed altar call; it was an important and special blessing that I will never forget.

At the time my mother was still alive but nearing the end and suffering from dementia. My sister Ruth and I went to her bedside in Texas and said to her, "Mother! It's okay now. You can go on to heaven. Juanita is waiting there for you." We knew she could not physically comprehend us, but we spoke to her spirit anyway. Mother did not pass away just then, but when she did, what a wonderful surprise waited for her on the other side!

I don't know if before I led Juanita in "the sinner's prayer" whether she was in danger of being eternally lost or whether she was in a place with God where she was in danger of losing eternal rewards. Since I could not know her heart at the time, I wanted her last prayer before she breathed her last breath on Earth to be a Yes to God by the simple blinking of the eyes. That she did. That night, I truly believe she had crossed over into Glory land. I would say to those who are praying for a spiritual awakening of a loved one, don't neglect to pray regardless of whether you know for sure their spiritual condition. Paul, in Colossians 1:9, wrote to believers and non-believers saying: "We do not cease to pray for you..."

4
Jerry!

Moses replied [to Pharoah], "We will all go—young and old, our sons and daughters, and our flocks and herds. We must join together in celebrating a festival to the Lord (Exodus 10:9 NLT).

At the time of my brother Jerry's lowest point away from God, he was a working alcoholic. We knew nothing about the extent of his drinking—which I find to be typical of alcoholics and many substance abusers. Our mother said to him, "Jerry, you can be bound by things that control you or be under someone else's control, but you can never be away from my spiritual authority in Christ. That authority enables me to take you before the Throne of God every time I pray."

What does a mother do when a good son messes up? My brother Jerry, like my sister Juanita, became a prodigal, but in a much different way than her. Jerry was the third sibling in the family after Juanita and David. Jerry seemed well adjusted, happy-go-lucky, and always had a funny joke to tell. He took me to my first professional baseball game at Forbes Field to watch the Pittsburg Pirates play the Brooklyn Dodgers. I honestly don't know if we had to sneak off to watch the game and not tell our parents. By then, it may have been that Mom and Dad had gotten detoxified from some of our household legalism. Jerry worked in a grocery store along with my brother David when they were fourteen and sixteen years old. This was a family necessity as they contributed to the overall finances, adding to the meager salary my dad received as a pastor. Sadly, neither of my brothers ever had the opportunity to enjoy normal teenage years. Every day after school they had to go to Harkins Market in an inner-city suburb of Pittsburg to work. Once, at the dinner table, my brothers asked Dad if they could stop working. He said, "Sons, we can't make it without the extra income you both bring in." I still recall the look on my Dad's face. It was so painful for him to tell them that.

At the age of seventeen, Jerry married a girl from the church that my father pastored in Turtle Creek, Pennsylvania. He was soon drafted into the Army and was stationed in Texas. His wife, Evelyn, joined him there at some point. It was there that Jerry naively got into trouble, drinking and gambling. The latter became an addiction. Then through circumstances for which I never knew (and frankly, didn't want to know), Jerry was given some type of discharge from the Army. He returned home and because of his previous experience working in a small supermarket, was qualified to be the Produce Manager in a larger supermarket.

Life seemed to be better for my brother as he and his wife gave birth to and raised four children. However, unbeknown to my parents and apparently my siblings as well, slowly Jerry's drinking got worse, and his wife made him leave their home. He moved in with another woman and that seemed to stabilize him. Then, over time, as is usually the case, the alcohol controlled him rather than it being controlled by him. Unfortunately for me, I was so busy helping build a ministry to drug addicts and alcoholics that I didn't have time to reach out to Jerry. I know my brother David kept monitoring Jerry's condition and where abouts. When David traveled as an evangelist, he would sometimes ask for prayer for Jerry.

Guilt in the Light

If you extend your soul to the hungry and satisfy the afflicted soul, then your light shall dawn in the darkness, and your darkness shall be as the noon day (Isaiah 58:10).

We can faithfully be walking in the Light of Christ and yet have blind spots to our possible part in a loved one's departure from the faith. If so, we need to let the light of God's forgiveness shine into our heart. I never discussed this with my brother David, but for myself there was a sense of guilt in that while helping hundreds come to Christ through Teen Challenge (the ministry we founded) our own dear brother desperately needed help to regain a spiritual awakening. It was as if the devil threw in our face what was said of Jesus on the cross: "He saved others, Himself He cannot save" (Mark 15:31).

Another type of guilt can be due to not having prayed faithfully for the spiritual awakening of a loved one. This can make you feel like you've lacked the faith to believe God can bring them back into relationship with Himself. I had more of this type of guilt being a sibling to two prodigals. I did not have the type of guilt some have in feeling that their prayers were the only means of saving a loved one.

Ultimately, the ironic good news for our family is that Jerry got worse. As hard as it can be to hear and accept, often the way up is first to go down—down into the mud and mire of sin (Psalm 40:1-2) The wayward one must come to a deep place of "want"—that is, wanting to change, wanting to be set free! This was the pattern with the son in the Parable of the Prodigal Son:

> But when he [the prodigal son] had spent all, there arose a famine in the land, and he began to be in want" (Luke 15:14).

"And he began to be in want." This is the key that caused the prodigal son to "come to himself"—finally admitting his sinful behavior was ruining his life—after which he said, "I will arise and go to my father" (Luke 15:17-18). The hardest part of faith for our wayward children is between the time they leave, and they want. They leave home, leave parents, spouse, and/or family, and leave the faith. At some point in their wanderings away, they begin to be in "want," a want that leads them home. And thankfully, it is a want of wanting a changed life. We *want* our loved ones to be in "want" sooner rather than later. Unfortunately, it's often later. This is why it's important to "leave the light on" for our prodigal loved ones, the light in our hearts of faith and hope expressed through our continued prayers. When praying as one like the father of the prodigal parable it is a wait, I call the in between time. In between "give me" and "forgive me."

In my brother's case, he wanted to reconnect with family again. So he called our sister Ruth who was a pastor's wife living in Long Island at the time. At the same time, Jerry was working in a high-end grocery store in Manhattan and living in Queens. I believe it was my brother David who encouraged Jerry to move to New York City to get closer to mother and family. He probably financed part of that move.

One Friday night Jerry showed up to our regular service we had in my early days as the Director of Teen Challenge, in Brooklyn. He'd come late and left the service early to avoid speaking to me. But it was one of Jerry's first steps back towards his spiritual awakening.

It is good for me to point out something I later learned from Jerry about his prodigal life. That is, he did not lose his faith in God. He simply quit practicing it. For example, when in a bar drinking and someone mocked God, the church, or especially preachers, he'd speak up in the defense of the things of God. Jerry was what we might call a follower of Jesus "from afar off." The drinking stood between him and his restoration. What was good for our family to know is that the Light of the Gospel of Jesus' delivering power shown strong in our faith and prayers. It was only dim in Jerry's life.

Faith is essential in praying for loved ones. In my mother's prayers, she often had "a word from the Lord." This is a strong feeling, a conviction, a spiritual impression of the mind and heart relative to the promises of God. I'm not sure which of the promises she was claiming, but it could be one of the following, which I encourage you to claim for your loved one:

- Proverbs 22:6: Train up a child in the way he should go, and when he is old, he will not depart from it.

- Point your kids in the right direction—when they're old they will not get lost (*The Message from the same verse above*).

- Matthew 21:22: Whatsoever things you ask in prayer, believing, you will receive.

5

Jerry's Homecoming

Then he called for a light, ran in, and fell down before Paul and Silas. And he brought them out and said, "Sirs, what must I do to be saved?" (Acts 16:30) Great shall the peace be of your children. In righteousness you shall be established (Isaiah 54:13-14).

The one verse of Scripture I heard repeated most often growing up in the church, relative to praying and believing for the prodigals of church members, is Acts 16:31:

> Believe on the Lord Jesus Christ, and you will be saved, you and your household.

"You and your household," is a promise that continued to reverberate in my soul and especially for my mother and brother David as well. This was a promise Paul and Silas shared with their jailor after the miracle of an earthquake took place, and their prison chains and bars were loosed. They could have then escaped but did not. This promise, given to the jailor, can be claimed by all believers praying for salvation of those in their own households.

In a church where my father pastored, on one occasion there were often many prayer requests for unsaved or backslidden loved ones. My father said, "Let's get serious in praying for loved ones." So, at one service he put a large poster on the wall in the sanctuary and told church members:

"Now put the names of those you're praying for on the wall poster." Then he said, "Lets believe our prayers will be answered. And when they are, go and drawn a line through that name." I shall never ever forget, over time, seeing various names having a line drawn through their name.

One Sunday morning, a man who faithfully attended the church but never claimed to have accepted Christ, just got up and went to the altar and confessed Jesus as his Lord and Savior. He simply said, "It was my time." I am sure his wife and the churches prayers brought this desire about. He became the father-in-law of my brother Jerry who married one of his daughters.

It soon came time for my brother Jerry to come back home to the Lord but let me put this special answer to prayer in an historical context. During the filming of the movie, *The Cross and Switchblade*—a film version of the bestselling book telling the story of the founding of Teen Challenge, the ministry my brother David Wilkerson and I co-founded—a scene was being made in Harlem. I visited the street where this was being filmed. My brother was portrayed by a former popular platinum recording artist, Pat Boone. Through not being known primarily for his acting roles, he was the catalyst behind the movie being made and thus earned the right to play my brother in the movie.

When I visited the streets in Harlem, I spoke to Pat Boone and asked if he would share a song at an upcoming Teen Challenge Rally to be held the same week on a Saturday night. Pat agreed to come and added, "My wife Shirley is flying in this weekend, and she will be with me." An expression I often heard growing up in the church was: "God works in mysterious ways, His wonders to perform." I forgot what verse this was actually based upon, but Isaiah 45:15 says, "Truly, O God of Israel, you work in mysterious ways."

The Good News in the Daily News

God used a two-inch advertisement I took out in a New York City Daily News newspaper advertising the Saturday night Gospel Rally. My brother Jerry saw this ad announcing the meeting which was to be held on 33rd Street off of 8th Avenue, of what then was a church called Glad Tidings Tabernacle. The ad simply gave the time and address of the meeting and stated: Speaker David Wilkerson. That name alone did not draw Jerry to the service, but I included in the advertisement, "Special Guest Pat Boone."

Now if you are not of mine or my brother's generation, the name "Pat Boone" probably would not mean anything to you. But it did to Jerry. Pat Boone was a popular pop singer of our generation in the 1950's and 60's, selling more than 45 million records and appearing in more than 12 Hollywood movies, including *The Cross And Switchblade*. The name Pat Boone drew Jerry to our rally.

As myself, my brother, Pat Boone, and his wife Shirley were in the Green Room preparing to go to the platform, my brother said, "Let's pray." At that very moment one of David's assistants entered the room and said, "Jerry is in the service." David briefly explained to the Boones about Jerry and then led in prayer for that evening's service, included Jerry in his prayer.

I was the MC of the meeting. On the very small platform were three people directly behind me. To my right was my brother David, and next to him Shirley Boone. There was nothing unusual about the beginning of the service which included Pat Boone and his wife singing a song for the congregation. I then introduced my brother David to speak. Before he left his seat, Shirley said to David, "I've been quietly praying all during the singing for your brother." She then just added four prophetic words: "Tonight is Jerry's night." My brother just looked at her, saying nothing. I believe a light went on in his heart at that moment. I believe, perhaps, that David wondered too if it was Jerry's homecoming night.

David went to the podium and read a Scripture and then just stood there, saying nothing. The congregation, including myself, looked at David and questioned what could be wrong and why he did not immediately begin preaching. Then, in a quiet, halting voice he said, "The Lord has laid a message on my heart, but I feel this is not the time or place to share it. Instead, I'm going to give an altar call to one person. Our brother Jerry is here in the meeting. Jerry, I know you're here. I see you. I know you're struggling. I want you to know our family has been praying for you. You are not an embarrassment to us. You are loved by us and by God." He said to the audience, "I'm going to make an altar call now for one person. Jerry, will you come back to God tonight?"

He did. He half ran; half walked down the aisle. There was a long altar rail all across the front of the church where Jerry knelt and called on God. David and I met him there. It was obvious by his brokenness that he had repented and cried out to God for mercy. Decades of prayers for Jerry were answered on this momentous, miraculous night for the Wilkerson household.

David then asked Jerry, "Do you want to go to our rehab place, the farm we have in Pennsylvania where others like yourself are learning to live a new life in Christ." He said, "Yes. I'm ready." My sister Ruth was in the audience that night, but our mother was not. My brother asked one of our Teen Challenge staff to drive Jerry to the Teen Challenge Training Center in Pennsylvania, but when they drove away from the church, Jerry asked Victor, the driver, if he would make a stop before they left the city: to Greenwich Village where we had an outreach coffee house called The Lost Coin. My mother and a co-worker ran that ministry, and that was the reason she was not at the Rally that evening.

Jerry walked through the door of the small room where there were tables set up to serve coffee to visitors walking off the streets, curious as to what The Lost Coin was all about. Besides coffee, the gospel was served through the conversations that occurred. At the moment Jerry stood in the doorway, our Mother was in the corner preparing a cup of coffee for a visitor. When she turned and saw him, the first words out of her mouth when seeing his smiling face was "Jerry, you came back to God tonight!" He said "Yes" and they embraced. Our prodigal had come home because the light of faith in my mother's heart had never gone out.

By late that night Jerry was in our Teen Challenge Training Center in Pennsylvania where he spent six months. He then returned home to his wife Eve and their four children. She also kept the Light of faith on for Jerry's homecoming even though I'm sure her faith was tested numerous times during my brother's time being separated from his family. It was a seven-year famine and separation between Jerry and his wife and their four children.

Jerry and Evelyn eventually moved to Texas where my brother had set up his ministry called World Challenge. Both worked for the ministry for decades and are now enjoying eternal fellowship with the rest of the extended Wilkerson family in heaven.

6

Walking and Praying in the Light

Giving thanks to the Father who has qualified us to be partakers of the inheritance of the saints in light (Colossians 1:12).

One praying mother said to her (backslidden) children, "You can get away from the church and away from home, but you can never, ever get away from my influence. As long as I can pray, I have power through the Spirit to see you return to the fold." This mother understood the principal of keeping the light on.

Some might contend that you can lead a horse to water, but you can't make them drink. It is never good to try to force a loved one to surrender to God. As believers, God has established parents as His appointed ministers in the redemption of a child. The sooner this happens, the better the long-term results. As children grow, they need to make their own choices regarding faith. It may or may not be the faith they were raised on.

Many parents come to Christ after a son and daughter has left home. In such cases the challenge is greater, but the promise of salvation to "you and your household" remains the same. In a daily devotional in *Our Daily Bread* the following was shared:

The sun never sets in Longyearbyen, Norway. Between mid-April to late August for about four months, the sun never goes down. You can take a sunny walk at 3 am because the sun is still up.

Every believer lives in the spiritual equivalent of Longyearbyen. Even at 3 a.m. we are still bathed with God's light. There is a song that says, "The morning is worth the midnight." I know many a mother that has spent nights in prayer for a son or daughter (or even a spouse) as they endeavor to walk in the light of faith for their loved one.

The study of light in the Bible is complex, for the term is used both physically and metaphorically. Light can symbolize many things, but chiefly it represents the presence of our holy, truthful, gracious God. (From Turning Points Daily Devotional, Sept. 2004)

Andrew Murray discusses parental power inherent in prayer:

We have, through the whole course of God's dealings with parents from Noah downward, seen that God gives the parent the right and the power to appear and act on behalf of the child, and that such representative action is accepted. To lay hold of this clearly is the very essence of parental faith; to act upon it is the secret of parental power and blessing. The whole family constitution is based on this. All the influence of being clear on this point: I am the steward of God grace to the children. I represent the child with God and am heard on his behalf. This makes him confident in saying I represent God with my child; I have God's help to give me influence and power. I have overcome the power of my child's sin and pleading with God for him (or her). I am sure conquering it in pleading with my child.[1]

Have believers and churches let the light of faith for a spiritual awakening of loved ones burn out; or worse, have we just turned off the light? I recall a time when my father, during a prayer meeting, would ask for a raise of hands of those who had an "unspoken prayer request." I knew that many of those silent, wordless prayer requests were for a backslidden loved one.

As previously shared, in one church in which my father was the Pastor, I saw a congregation put faith and action into their theology. They literally walked in the light of faith through prayer for loved ones. They began a concentrated effort of intercessory prayer to reach the unsaved loved ones of the church members. Someone made a chart with the names of those being prayed for. Never a service past without making mention of them before the throne of God.

Also, special prayer times were held for the specific purpose of presenting before the Lord that list of names. Then, as the Lord began to answer those prayers, what joy it was to see the converted loved one go to the back of the church, take a pen or pencil in hand, and cross their names off the list. They too then joined the ranks of prayers. I learned out of that experience that when a group of people get desperate and mean business with God, they get results.

Many years ago, one father, whose son had strayed from the Lord, went to a shed behind his house and sought the Lord for the salvation of his prodigal son. With Bible in hand, he would open it up to Acts 16:31, put his finger on the verse and say, "Lord, this is Your Word. I am standing on it for (then naming his son). After years of such praying and pointing, he wore a hole in that page of the Bible where was written: "Believe on the Lord Jesus Christ and thou shalt be saved, and thy household."

Finally, his prayer was answered. This man's son served as a remarkable missionary in South Africa for many years. I traveled with that missionary on one occasion, and he told me that when his father came across the hole in the page where Acts 16:31 was no longer readable, he simply lifted his heart in praise to God for the answered prayer.

Testimonies abound as to the results of parents, wives, husbands, families, members, and friends, having prayed for the spiritual awakening of loved ones, just as my sister Juanita and my brother Jerry returned to God and had spiritual awakenings as a result of our family prayers.

I suggest at this point you take a Prayer Pause to pray for your own prodigal loved ones! Here is a sample powerful prayer confession for parents and loved ones:

Blessed Son of God, in mercy I come before You for (name the person or persons you are praying for) that are living a life void of Your peace and presence, unconverted and under the power of the evil one. Oh Lord Jesus, have compassion on us and help us. Let_____ be delivered from Satan's power. Oh, make him or her a child of God. I have to confess that at times how little my life has been a life of faith and how unbelief has entered and kept me from praying and believing our family prodigal would wake up and regain the desire to know You. I want to commit to lifting up my loved ones to You in faith that a desire for You will be lit like a flame in their heart. May they open themselves to Your will in their lives and accept you as their Lord and Savior.

If you have trusted the Lord for the salvation of your soul, God's promises extend to your entire family. This I know for sure, as it is what happened to my siblings. Someone said, "How can you make such a bold claim for the salvation of loved ones based on that one scripture in Acts 16:31? After all, this was a promise made to just one man, the jailor and his family. That is true. However, the promise of salvation to whole households is a thread that is weaved throughout the entire Bible.

Here are further Scriptures that reflect these promises:

- I will pour out my Spirit on your descendants, and my blessings on your offspring (Isaiah 44:3).

- My righteous will be forever, and My salvation from generation to generation (Isaiah 51:8).

- The promise is to you and your children, and to all who are afar off, as many as the Lord shall call (Acts 2:39).

Note how frequently throughout Scripture these words appear:

- "You and your household."
- "You and your seed."
- "You and your children."
- "Me and my house."

These Scriptures also talk about God calling people who are "afar off" to Himself:

- Isaiah 33:13: Hear you who are afar off, what I have done; And you who are near, acknowledge my might.

- Luke 17: 12-14: Then as He entered a certain village, there met Him ten lepers, who stood afar off. And they lifted up their voices and said, "Jesus, Master, have, mercy on us!"…They were cleansed.

All the Old Testament promises to "you and your seed" were fulfilled in the first coming of Christ and in the outpouring of the Holy Spirit on the day of Pentecost. Peter said that through repentance everyone can be "baptized in the name of Jesus Christ for the remission of sins" (Acts 2:38).

7

The Olive Tree Promise

But I am like a green olive tree in the house of God; I trust in the mercy of God forever and ever (Psalm 52:8).

In the Holy Land, from the time of King David onward, if a family had olive trees, it was a sign of the blessing of the Lord. Olives were a commodity that if one had in abundance, they provided an adequate living. They could earn an even better living from the sale of the oil than from harvesting the olives.

> The olive touched nearly every phase of Jewish life. Olive wood was used for carpentry, and the fruit served as food. And the oil found its way into a variety of medicines and ointments, as well as fuel for light. (KJV Study Bible)[2]

It was probably olive oil that the father of the prodigal son used when he left the light on in his window when he retired for the evening just in case his son returned in the darkness of the night. I love olives. My wife knows I always want some in our refrigerator. Besides loving olives for the taste, they are a reminder to me of my three adult children and five grandchildren when I read Psalm 128 verse 3 in the NLT. It says, *"Your children will be like vigorous young olive trees as they sit around your table."* Being blessed with children in a God-fearing family was to have even a greater blessing. When I pray for the faith-strayers and prodigals in my extended family, I am reminded of this "Olive Tree Promise" from Psalm 128.

I remind you of this promise as well, when you pray for the spiritual awakening of your loved ones. I pray regularly for several families whose children do not speak to their mother and some siblings who do not speak to each other. As I pray, I often reread Psalm 128. In one such family, I know they claim to be children of God, but they are not living biblically as they should as a family. I pray for all individuals involved that they would have a spiritual awakening and come to an awakening to the truth that says, "Love one another." I know many families that do not "Sit around the table" as is promised in Psalm 128.

My prayer for you who are reading this is to claim the Olive Tree Promise for yourself. David used the image of an Olive Tree as a sign of being able to stand in the house of the Lord as one "steadfast in God" (See Psalm 82:8 KJV). The Psalmist writes in Psalm 128 a song of worship portraying this imagery and promise of God as a family sitting under an Olive Tree being "rich with [spiritual] healthy children." May all who pray for the "spiritual awakening" of their loved ones be blessed with the answer to this promise.

I use the term "spiritual awakening" to describe various types of relationships that men and women have with God and in turn, with Jesus Christ. These types are as follows:

1. Those who have never shown they are followers of Jesus in any way. In a word, they are the "unsaved."

Whosoever shall call on the name of the Lord shall be saved (Romans 10:13).

As you pray, for your unsaved loved ones, use this scripture and put the name of the person you're praying for in the place of "whosoever."

2. Those who have grown up in a God-fearing home in which church attendance was required. But when they came to "the age of accountability" they never walked in the fear of God. They chose to follow the path of the Broad Road that leads to destruction.

The first Spiritual Awakening recorded in the Bible is found in Genesis 4:9: "At that time people began to call on the name of the Lord." It was a sovereign work of God that this spiritual awakening took place. Pray in faith that God will continue to sovereignly draw your loved ones to a place where they "call on the name of the Lord."

3. Those who grew up with a God-fearing parent or parents who received the teachings of the Bible which affected them in a good way; in that they live by good moral values, but they were never born-again.

Romans 8:7 says, "Being descendants of Abraham doesn't make them truly Abraham's children." Being raised in the church and a God-fearing family often results in the children inheriting good moral values but being "good" is not good enough to qualify for heaven. My sister Juanita often boasted saying, "I'm a good person." She was, but growing up "Wilkerson" did not mean she was truly following in the faith in which she grew up. This type, we might call the good prodigals. Yet, they can be an even greater challenge than the type of prodigal spoken of in the Parable of the Prodigal Son. He was the son of his father, but he needed to surrender to *the Father* in heaven, which he did.

4. Those whose lives are more like the biblical prodigal but end up at rock bottom as an alcoholic, drug addict, and in some cases, a criminal.

Your loved one might be described as one who "sat in darkness, in utter darkness, prisoners suffering in chains" and were "at their wit's end" (Psalm 107:10 and 27). *Wits* has to do with having a sound mind. "Wit's end' is when a person ends up having lost all hope. It is to the parents and family that I especially write to and invite you to send the names of these individuals to Brooklyn Teen Challenge for our students and staff—most of them former prodigals themselves— to pray for your prodigal (See Chapter 11).

5. Another category that should be included are the "backsliders."

The nation of Israel was full of serial backsliders. Over and over again we read the prophets of God using their voice to call back backsliders to Him, such as in Jeremiah 3:22: "Return, you backsliding children, and I will heal your backslidings. Indeed, we do come to You, for You are the Lord our God." Throughout all the major and minor prophets this same truth is repeated over and over with warnings of judgement followed by God's call of a spiritual awakening.

Your loved ones in need of a spiritual awakening may fall under one of these categories, but there are multitudes who have experienced religion in various way, but not salvation. I was a co-pastor at Times Square Church on Broadway from the mid 1980's to the mid 90's. Scores of people answered the call to give their lives to Christ who had what I call a cultured and religious type of faith but had never been born again. When they heard the full gospel message we preached, dozens in almost every service, answered the call to surrender to God's will for their lives to experience salvation and conversion. In Jesus' day, there were many Israelites who called Abraham the father of their faith but rejected Jesus as the Messiah. They were unwilling to pay the cost of becoming one of His disciples, the Giver of Salvation.

If you have not been keeping the Light of faith on in your prayers and your heart for the spiritual awakening of your loved ones, then begin now. Here are three sample prayers you can use to help you begin praying for them.

Sample Prayer One. A Scripture and a prayer for a loved one raised in a godly, church-going family

The love of the Lord remains forever with those who fear him. His salvation extends to the children's children (Psalm 103:17 NLT).

Because I fear the Lord and because I have received salvation, my child is promised salvation. It is his [and her] birthright and is theirs for the asking. Jesus, this promise says your Love is eternally with my family. Reveal your love to _____.

Lord, wherever he [or she] is and whatever he/she is doing, please remind him/her they are a child of the Most High God. Help him/her to remember their childhood fondly, how they loved going to church, singing songs to You, hearing stories about You, and being around Your people. May he/she yearn for the God of their childhood.

Today, I declare the promise of the children's children: one day _____will be saved!

Sample Prayer Two

Now all glory to God, who is able to keep you from falling away and will bring you with great joy into his glorious presence without a single fault (Jude 1:24 NLT).

Lord, this promise from Jude puts me in a mood to praise You! One day _____ will choose to surrender their life to You. They will break free of their chains and will serve You faithfully until the final day. I see him/her entering Your throne room…not with head down in shame, but with eyes bright, looking to the One they adore. They will not be found guilty of a single thing. Right now, they are drowning in muck and mire, but on that day they will walk tall, eager to receive their rewards as a rightful heir. Please give him/her a divine glimpse into their future. I ask that even now he/she experiences Your glorious presence. Today I declare that someday Jesus will present _____to the Father with great joy. Heaven will celebrate!

Sample Prayer Three

(Note: This prayer is taken directly from the book, *Promises for Prodigals* by Lori Wilkerson Stewart.)[3]

Our children will also serve Him (Psalm 22:30a).

Father, I am your faithful follower. Serving You has been my greatest joy and delight. Knowing You gives my life significance and meaning. I want the same for _____. He [she] is floundering out there; a young man [woman] full of gifts, talents, and abilities, but sin robbed him [her] of any real purpose in life.

This Psalm this first promises that my future seed, my tribe, [and]my prosperity is destined to serve You. I believe in generational blessings; Your word says You maintain lovingkindness for a thousand generations to those who love and obey You (Deuteronomy 7:9). How great is your faithfulness!

Today, I declare that one day _____ will serve You.

8

Mothers and Others Who Kept the Light On

Pay close attention, friend, to what your father tells you; never forget what you learned at your mother's knee. Wear their counsel like a winning crown, like rings on your fingers (Proverbs 1:8 The Message Bible).

Some of the greatest prayer warriors I have known have been mothers, grandparents, spouses, siblings and other family members who have prayed through long seasons for the spiritual awakening of the ones they love in the Lord (and in the flesh). In the long list of hard-fought victories won by prayer, I rank at the top mothers and others who kept the light of faith on in their hearts for their loved one. These moms are found in the Scriptures, as well as today in their War Rooms of prayer. Prayers for our prodigals are often the greatest challenge as we wrestle in prayer until the answer comes. I will share examples of mothers I have personally known (one being my own mom) as well as some mothers in the Bible who did the same.

One of my favorites is Mrs. Torres. When she, her husband, and their two sons immigrated from Puerto Rico to Brooklyn the family's dream of a new life turned into a nightmare when their oldest son Victor became a hardcore heroin addict. As soon as she learned the depth of her son's problem, she engaged in serious intercessory prayer for

Victor. She then asked her small storefront Spanish Pentecostal congregation to pray for her wayward son as well.

She'd plead with the Lord, often declaring to Him, "Lord, my son does not belong to the devil. He belongs to you!" She never gave up hope that one day this would become a reality. She would even go looking for him in the streets. One day she was divinely led as she found Victor on a rooftop about to be thrown off some ten stores to his death by a group of guys. She intervened and saved his life.

She knew that only God could save his soul and deliver him from drugs. She heard about a Christian program called "Teen Challenge" in Brooklyn and she sort of tricked Victor in going, telling him this place was "offering a new kind of cure." She was not exactly lying, as in fact, at the time there was no other such faith-based drug treatment offering a new kind of cure by introducing addicts to Jesus Christ! She left that part out while begging Victor to come to Teen Challenge. When he woke up the first morning after staying the night and heard singing from the chapel—just like the worship in his mother's church—Victor said, "Oh, no! My mother tricked me. I'm in a hallelujah program!" But he stayed and in a short time, Mrs. Torres' prayers were answered. I became his pastor, counselor, mentor, and we have remained good friends over the many years since his spiritual transformation.

Teen Challenge became like an ark of safety for Victor, like baby Moses of old being saved from drowning in the waters of death. Do you remember Jochebed, the mother of Moses? When the Pharoah in Egypt saw the Jews flourishing and multiplying, he decided they were a threat to his rule, so he commanded all the male babies of the Israelites to be put to death. Jochebed refused to allow her newborn son to be lost to her, lost to God, and lost to finding his life's purpose and destiny. For his first three months, she hid him. Did she do so with fear? Oh my goodness, what mother would not have? Did she pray during those days? Yes, privately and silently as she also had to keep Moses from crying out. His future destiny was to cry out for the deliverance of his people from their cruel Egyptian bondage. God used a miniature ark to save Moses as he was placed in it and then sent down the Nile River into the household of Pharoah and his daughter. (See Exodus, Chapters 1 and 2) I compare Mrs. Torres with Jochebed in that she found a place of safety for Moses in constructing that miniature Noah's ark to save him.

The Wife Who Never Gave Up On Her Husband

Many people whom I have had the blessing of helping find freedom in Christ from alcoholism and addiction had first lost everything: careers, homes, health, family, and spouses. Often addiction breaks apart marriages that are never healed. I recall the wife of a young man in his twenties, married for five to six years. His spouse brought him his clothes one day. I talked with her as I reached into the trunk of her car to get the luggage filled with his clothes.

I asked her, "Is there any possibility that when he completes recovery that you will accept him back?"

Very calmly she answered, "Reverend, I'm sorry, but he's put me though so much sorrow and pain that I just don't have it in me to forgive him."

And with that she drove off. I didn't want to tell this husband his marriage was over, for I had seen in other similar situations a miracle take place, and the marriage was healed.

This brings me back to the story of my brother Jerry and the rest of our story. Jerry's drinking got him banished from his house, his marriage, and his four children. Romans 12:18 (KJV) says, "If it is possible, as much as depends on you, live peaceably with all men." When it applies to a marriage, I have always interpreted that phrase "as much as depends on you" that some who are not willing to even try to repair a marriage damaged by addiction. Most do not. My brother Jerry's wife Eve was one of the rare ones.

After leaving home Jerry at some point sought a divorce from Eve but she did not give it to him. I don't know all the circumstances as to why she did not want a divorce, but I do believe it was because in her upbringing marriage was "until death do us part." I did meet Jerry's new girlfriend at one point, and she was courteous to her and my brother. Even she eventually cut Jerry loose for the same reason his wife did—his drinking made him an unfit companion. When Jerry ended up in our Pennsylvania Teen Challenge Training Center, I was so pleased to learn that he became a part of a student-led monthly prayer meeting for those who prayed for their spouses, asking the Lord to heal their marriages.

One weekend my brother was assigned by Teen Challenge to visit a church in the suburbs of Pittsburg in which he, among other students, were to give their testimony. When they drove up the church for a Sunday service, to my brother's surprise, it was just a few blocks from his estranged wife. When he told this to his fellow students, they said, "You've gotta go see her!" He thought he might not be welcomed. That Sunday afternoon my brother was praying, and he felt a voice inside him say, "Go home!" So he did—with fear and trembling.

When Eve came to the door, she simply said, "Welcome home, Jerry." That was the beginning of Jerry's restoration of his marriage and to his family. I have written this in other books entitled *The Grace of God* and *Two Sides of the Door*. The same grace that healed Jerry's relationship to God was also unbeknown to him, working in his wife. She had heard that Jerry was in Teen Challenge and followed his progress from a distance. At one point, she gathered her children together to prepare them for their father's possible homecoming and that they all were to make it as smooth as possible. Eventually Jerry and Eve moved to Texas where they both worked in my brother David's ministry organization.

The Young Man with a Vulgar Past
Who Became a Bishop—Because of His Mother's Prayer

The name Saint Augustine of Hippo may not be on the top of your list of heroes of faith in the early church, but he is on my list. Here we find another example of the godly, praying mother of Saint Augustine named Monica. Augustine eventually became a Catholic theologian, philosopher, and Bishop in North Africa between 354-430 AD. His was made famous through his best-selling book, *The City of God*. Any serious historian of early church history would, as I have, used quotes from his famous writings. He was one of ancient history's most influential bishops and defender of the Christian faith.

His past life was one who was a prodigal, having been raised by his godly mother Monica who lovingly and persistently prayed for decades for his return to the faith after he had been living many years in gross immorality. Augustine said in his own words about his life of wickedness: "I could not distinguish between the shining light of affection and the darkness of lust…I could not keep within the kingdom of light, where friendship binds soul to soul…and so I polluted the brook of friendships with the sewage of lust."

Augustine's mother Monica knew her son had fallen deep into the pit of iniquity. And to make matters worse, he became a disciple of a cult of that era, a double blow to his mother. But still she had hope, strong hope because of her prayers. Monica stayed firm in her belief that one day all things would work together for the good of her son and herself. This conviction was boosted by a vision she had from the Lord in which she saw Augustine as a shining youth running towards her like the prodigal returning to the father in Jesus' parable. In the vision she saw her son cheerful and smiling towards her, asking what the reason for her grief was. She replied that she was "bewailing his state of perdition" and that if he continued on his current path, he would suffer eternal damnation. At one point a bishop who Monica sought counsel from said to her, "Go, go! Leave it alone. Live on as you are living. It is not possible that the son [of the mother] of such tears should be lost." So, it was to be as the bishop said.

Augustine had left home in spite of his mother's pleas that he not go. He wanted to go to Rome. It was there in the divine providence of God and by the grace of God and the conviction of the Holy Spirit the light of truth he had been taught from his mother came shining bright as a laser beam into his mind and heart.

Ruth Bell Graham wrote:

Augustine would go on to more than fulfill all his godly mother's hopes and prayers, becoming a bishop and defender of the truth. Having him come home at last, this prodigal would help build a house of faith that stands to this day.[4]

In the words of Malcolm Muggeridge,

Thanks largely to Augustine, the light of the New Testament did not go out with Rome's [downfall] but remained amidst debris of the fallen empire to light a way to another civilization, Christianity.[5]

As for Monica, her work on earth was almost done. One day, shortly after Augustine's conversion, she announced to him that she had nothing left to live for, now that she had achieved her lifelong quest of seeing him come to faith in Christ. Just nine days later, she died.

John Newton, the Famous Hymn Writer and His Mother's Prayers

John Newton not only wrote one of the most famous hymns in history, *"Amazing Grace"* but he also experienced amazing grace in his life. Ruth Bell Graham wrote,

Though fragile in body, John Newton's mother was strong in spirit...Like Hannah with little Samuel, she taught John thoroughly. Grounded him in the Scriptures [Elizbeth], taught him to love them. They memorized portions together. She taught him hymns and the catechism. John responded early. Unlike other boys his age, he enjoyed studying more than playing. By the time he was four, he could read fluently.[6]

At the age of seven John Newton's mother died. Her work was done, but Satan's began. John went through a turbulent childhood, trying to live with purpose and in the godly ways his mother taught him. He joined the Royal Navy seeking to find himself and his life's purpose. On the seas he ended up in North Africa a slave of a black women married to a degenerate white slave-owner named Crow. She humiliated him and for two years even deprived him of a normal diet. Newton escaped from this enslavement and unfortunately began to traffic in slave-trading, the best way to make a living as a ship captain. He went from bad to worse. He readily admitted being an infidel and went against all social and moral standards of that time. He out-cursed the worst of sailors. Even other hardened ship captains knew John as a Jonah. Whenever and wherever he was hired as a ship's mate trouble followed him; and even the ship he was on encountered problems.

One day, like Jonah, a violent storm made the ship he was on like a death-trap. Newton cried out for mercy. It was to be the beginning of God's mercy to save his soul and at the time to save his life. Newton said of this transformation that he knew from his Jonah-like survival of a life-threatening storm that it was God's doing. After that his life gradually changed. Newton said it was God's mercy that saved his mom from having to endure his years as a prodigal. He felt undeserving of God's grace. Ruth Graham wrote that, "Newton continued in the slave-trading after conversion. At that time it was considered as respectable business." But then the Holy Spirit convicted him, and he gave up the sea, and for nine years worked in the custom house in Liverpool.

He ended up in London by some circumstances unknown and began a weekly prayer meeting there. He persuaded his friend William Cowper to attend, who later became a famous poet and hymn writer. Together they wrote hymns for use in the prayer meeting and one of them was Amazing Grace. It was said Newton used the tune based on one he learned from the slaves he used to traffic in. Some said the sounds almost seem wrung from the hearts of slaves in their suffering.

My prayer for those reading this is that one day they too will see God's amazing grace come to pass for their loved ones being praying for. When and if a spiritual awakening happens, especially if it's a mother's prayer, this can be a second experience of joy similar to the physical birth of their child. The Bible says that when a loved one is saved after never having been born-again or being a backslider and they come to the Lord, it is a time of great joy:

> Those who sow with tears will reap with songs of joy. Those who go out weeping, carrying seed to sow, will return with songs of joy, carrying sheaves with them (Psalm 126:5 NIV).

9

The Most Difficult Question:
Are All The Children In?

I think ofttimes as the night draws nigh
of an old house on the hill,
of a yard all wide and blossom-starred
where the children played at will.

And when the night at last came down,
hushing the merry din,
Mother would look around and ask,
"Are all the children in?"

'Tis many and many a year since then,
and the old house on the hill
no longer echoes to childish feet,
and the yard is oh, so still.

But I see it all, as the shadows creep,
and though many the years have been
since then, I can hear Mother ask,
"Are all the children in?"

I wonder if, when the shadows fall
on the last short earthly day,
when we say good-bye to the world outside,
all tired with our childish play,

When we step out into that other land
where Mother so long has been,
will we hear her ask, just as of old,
"Are all the children in?"[7]

M y good friend the Reverend Ed Spinola and I stood in the chilly October winds of a Long Island, New York cemetery. The undertaker waited as I had the grim task of conducting a brief committal ceremony for three burned, charred bodies; a father, a mother, and a two- year-old baby. As the caskets were lowered into the gravesite, I recalled the events leading to their lonely and tragic deaths.

Some weeks prior, I had received a letter from a Christian couple out West. "Would you look up relatives of ours living in Lower Manhattan? They're both addicts and they have a young child. Perhaps you could talk to them about going into Teen Challenge," the letter stated. I sent one of our workers to the address supplied. No one was home. A second visit still found them away. Information about where we could be contacted if they wanted help, and a booklet entitled, *A Positive Cure to Drug Addiction* were left, but no contact was made.

Then I received a call from the distant couple telling me the tragic news of their relatives' deaths. "Would you please go to the cemetery and conduct a simple committal ceremony?" the gentleman asked. He explained the circumstances surrounding the deaths. Apparently, there had been no heat in the apartment; a situation which is not unusual in New York City projects.

So, they started a fire in a wastebasket. Draperies caught on fire, and the three perished in the flames which engulfed the entire place. Although my encounter with the Christian couple was brief and although I never met the drug- addicted relatives or the child, I have often wondered about their reaction to the untimely deaths. Apparently, the addicted couple did not know the Lord Jesus Christ as their personal Savior and died without hope either in this life, or the life to come.

There have been other difficult burials and funerals over the years of working with troubled and addicted youth and adults. The dual tragedy is the physical death of a loved one coupled with the bereavement of the living. When the bereavement includes sorrow over the fact that the loved one died "in trespasses and sins," it raises those difficult questions. "Was my son/daughter ready to meet the Lord?" "Will I meet my loved ones in heaven?" "If they were not saved, won't there then be tears in heaven?"

I have seen good Christian families crushed by the troubles, sins, and waywardness of their children. I have seen pastors nearly forced to leave a church and community because of the wickedness of a child or children. It has been said, "Children are doubtful blessings." How true! What a blessing are children who serve the Lord and follow the Christian example of their parents.

> As arrows are in the hands of a mighty man; so are children of the youth. Happy is the man that has his quiver full of them: they [the parents] shall not be ashamed, [especially when the arrows are going straight by following the Lord] but they shall speak with the enemies [unsaved] in the gate [neighborhood and community] (Psalm 127:4, 5 Amplified Bible).

If those arrows turn away from Christ, they can be destructive not only to themselves, but to the testimony, unity, joy, and blessing of the home.

Charles Spurgeon wrote:

No cross is so heavy to carry as a living cross. Next to a woman who is bound to an ungodly husband or a man who is unequally yoked with a graceless wife, I pity the father whose children are not walking in the truth; who yet is himself an earnest Christian. Must it always be so, that the father shall go to the house of God and his son to the Alehouse? Shall the father sing songs of Zion, and the son and daughter pour forth ballads of Belial? Must we come to the communion table alone, and our children separated from us? Must we go on the road to holiness and the way of peace, and behold our dearest ones traveling with the multitude the broad way, despising what we prize, rebelling against Him whom we adore? God grant it may not be so, but it is a very solemn reflection. Most solemn still is the vision before us if we cast our eyes across the river of death into the eternity beyond. What if our children should not walk in the truth, and should die unsaved? There cannot be tears in heaven; but if there might, the celestials would look over the bulwarks of the New Jerusalem and weep their fill at the sight of their children in the flames of hell, forever condemned, forever shut out from hope. What if those to whom we gave being should be weeping and gnashing their teeth in torment while we are beholding the face of our Father in heaven? Remember, the separation time must come.[8]

What comfort can be offered to Christians who have lost an unsaved loved one through death? What comfort had King David when he "went up to the chamber over the gate, and wept. And as he went, he said thus: 'O my son Absalom—my son, my son Absalom—if only I had died in your place! O Absalom my son, my son!'" (2 Samuel 18:33)

Charles Spurgeon, in the previously quoted passage, went on to relate that he was greeted at a funeral of a parishioner's daughter by the father who whispered the following words to him:

> The worst of all is, sir, we have no evidence of conversion. We would have gladly parted with the dear one if we might have had some token for good. It breaks my wife's heart, sir. Comfort her if you can.

Spurgeon's message continues:

> I have felt that I was a poor comforter, for to sorrow without hope is to sorrow indeed. I pray it may never be the lot of any one of us to weep over our grown-up sons and daughters dead and twice dead. Better were it that they had never been born, better they had perished like untimely fruit, than that they should live to dishonor their father's God and their mother's Savior, and then should die to receive, "Depart, ye cursed," from those very lips which to their parents will say, "Come ye blessed of My Father, inherit the kingdom prepared for you." Proportionate to the greatness of the joy before us is the terror of the contrast. I pray devoutly that such an overwhelming calamity

may never happen to anyone connected with any of our families.

But such a calamity does happen. We cannot—we must not—ignore it. All too often I have been in the company of a bereaved family, listening to another minister saying glowing words about the departed one, offering hope for his or her salvation, where—possibly—no hope exists. But who is to judge the departed one? Certainly not the minister; or the family; or friends. It is within the divine providence of the Lord, alone. What remains for us, the living, is to comfort the bereaved, and to offer them the assurance that God's will— His just and right will—prevails at all times and in all matters. Such an occasion and circumstance should serve to remind us of that day when we meet the Master, to make ready our own preparation.

We cannot assure a Christian family that a loved one is with the Lord when, in fact, there is no basis or evidence of conversion. There are occasions when a person's relationship with Christ is unknown. In such cases, there is always the hope that the departed had made peace with God. I have known an individual who gave little or no appearance of faith in Christ because he did not fit the typical pattern of the evangelical believer. He used none of the jargon which is characteristic of the stereotyped evangelical. But I also knew the person to love the Lord, to pray secretly, to read the Bible on rare occasions. That person, I am sure, I will see when I cross Jordan. We can judge a person unjustly regarding his relationship to Christ.

But in cases where it is clearly known the person had not yielded his will to Christ, we cannot gloss over it. "He who believes in Him is not condemned; but he who does not believe is condemned already, because he has not believed in the name of the only begotten Son of God" (John 3:18). As strong as our love for our family may be, our love for the truth must be stronger. If our own flesh and blood are judged by the Word and therefore are "weighed in the balances and found wanting," (Daniel 5:27), our faith must outweigh our feelings. If our children "perish," then "let God be true, but every man a liar" (Romans 3:4).

I believe when Christians get to heaven and stand at the Judgment Seat of Christ, we will be so satisfied with the righteous judgment, justice, and holiness of our Lord that any sadness over missing loved ones will be wiped away in the joy of knowing a sovereign God has exercised judgment according to truth. An earthly illustration might help. Suppose your child had committed a crime for which you knew he was guilty. At the sentencing, you would be saddened and heartsick to hear the judge say to him, "I commit you to three years in the state prison." As you watched your child being taken into custody, you might find hope in only one thing: justice had been done. That is the way the system works. A man is innocent until proven guilty; but when convicted, the law and justice require that the criminal must pay. Our courts, judges, juries, trials, and jails all testify to the American way of justice. It does not always work as our founding fathers intended it, but it's the best system we have.

God operates His laws and His kingdom with no less justice. The same Word that saves, condemns. We must subscribe to it regardless of who is judged by it. In heaven, we will rejoice in the fact that our sovereign God has reigned in righteousness.

But we are sure that the judgment of God is according to truth against them which commit such things (Romans 2:2).

Far be it from You to do such a thing as this, to slay the righteous with the wicked, so that the righteous should be as the wicked; far be it from You! Shall not the Judge of all the earth do right? (Genesis 18:25)

Whatever God does with our loved ones, we can rest assured that He has done right. In eternity everything else will be overshadowed by this fact. We will worship Him throughout eternity for His righteousness. As the hymn states:

> *Turn your eyes upon Jesus*
> *Look full in His wonderful face*
> *and the things of earth will grow strangely dim*
> *in the light of His glory and grace.*

Behold, the Lord comes with ten thousands of His saints, to execute judgment on all, to convict all who are ungodly among them of all their ungodly deeds which they have committed in an ungodly way, and of all the harsh things which ungodly sinners have spoken against Him (Jude 14, 15).

Many verses throughout the Book of Revelation give us a picture of how our worship of Christ will seemingly eradicate the tears we have known in this life. Not even the absence of loved ones can take away the glory of life in the new world. We will be busy, for example, singing such things as "the song of Moses the servant of God, and the song of the Lamb, saying, 'Great and marvelous are Your works, Lord God Almighty! Just and true are Your ways, O King of the saints!'" (Revelation 15:3) We will hear heavenly creatures who rest neither day nor night saying, "Holy, holy, holy, Lord God Almighty, which was, and is, and is to come" (Revelation 4:8).

It is difficult to explain or understand fully how we in heaven will view displeasing events on earth, or how we will receive the unpleasant thought of eternal separation from loved ones. We live on this side of heaven. Now "we see in a mirror, dimly, but then face to face" (1 Corinthians 13:12). We know not what it is like to view events from "the other side." I am sure the perspective from that side will be so glorious, so wonderful, so beautiful, so awesome, that there will truly be "no tears in heaven." In this life we have questions. In the life to come, we will have answers.

We'll understand and say, "Well done, Lord."

10

Grandparents Who Keep the Light On

Let the children [and grandchildren] come to me. Don't stop them. For the kingdom of God belongs to these who are like these children (Luke 18:16 NLT).

A friend who works in a faith-based, Christ-centered rehab program shared with me, "Brother Don, I have discovered that some of the greatest unsung heroes of the faith are African American grandmothers in the inner cities. So many of our residents who accept Christ and see their lives changed have praying grandmothers who never stopped believing for the salvation of their kids and grandkids." This is a direct fulfillment of Bible promises, such as the following:

The mercy of the Lord is from everlasting to everlasting on those who fear Him, and His righteousness to children's children (Psalm 103:17).

Psalm 128:6 (in The Message Bible) encourages God's people to:

Enjoy the good life in Jerusalem [meaning the place and center of worship such as the church] every day of your life. And enjoy your grandchildren.

Proverbs 13:22 says, "A good man leaves an inheritance to his children's children." What greater inheritance can parents and grandparents leave to their children and grandchildren then to keep the light of faith and prayer on for the spiritual awakening of their children and children's children.

Many of the grandmother's praying for their lost loved ones are by no means financially well off, yet what they do have and know is the God who promises blessings to their grandchildren or 'children's children' as the Bible refers to grandchildren. I think of the grandmother who said, "My son's son ironically has rebelled against his father's rejection of Christianity by becoming a born-again Christian." At least that's how this grandmother viewed her grandson's faith in Christ. I have seen it happen in numerous families of sons and daughters that turned away from the Lord, but the grandchildren turned towards the Lord.

For all grandparents and loved ones praying for someone they love who has yet to have their spiritual awakening, here are some points to consider— especially if you are the grandparent praying for a grandchild.

Three Things to Do When Your Prayers for Grandchildren Seem to Go Unanswered

1. Practice Radical Acceptance.

The quickest way to relieve overwhelming emotions is to practice radical acceptance. According to mental health professional Marsha Linehan,

> Radical acceptance is a practice that helps us evaluate situations and work to reduce the emotional burden of the reality of the situation like resentment, anger, hatred, or shame.[9]

Being accepting of a fact of life does not mean being a person who thinks 'whatever will be will be.' Not at all. For a believer an unanswered prayer takes faith to leave the matter in God's hand and accept things as they are while at the same time trusting God who does all things well. Acceptance enables you to move forward in faith because:

> God has made everything beautiful for His own time. He has planted eternity in the human heart, but even so, people cannot see the scope of God's work from beginning to end (Ecclesiastes 3:11 NLT).

I recall my sister Juanita's (Nan) homecoming to the Lord on her death bed. After it happened, the first thought in my mind was how much I wanted to go and tell my mother the miracle that had taken place for which she had prayed for Nan for decades. Then, I realized because of mom's dementia she would not be able to experience the joy of Nan's spiritual awakening. My sister Ruth and I did go to our mother's bed side and said to her; "mother you can go now (meaning to heaven) Juanita will be waiting for you over there."

I tell this story to encourage praying parents and grandparents that they may not see the answer to their prayers for a loved one in this life, but they should keep hope alive that they may meet the answer to their prayer in heaven. I think one of the surprises of heaven will be to see the child or grandchild you have been praying for embrace the Lord, as Ecclesiastes 3:11 says we in this life cannot "see the beginning to the end."

2. Keep Knocking!

I have witnessed the sadness and the broken heartedness of those whose sons and daughters, or grandsons and granddaughters live in spiritual darkness. I've heard their question, "What can I do for my son or daughter?"

Those who know about the dramatic life changes of a dope addict, alcoholic, or person with a life-controlling problem will often approach me and briefly share a word about their child or grandchild's problem. The private grief and daily burden of these mothers and fathers, and in some cases of grandparents, leave me at a loss for words of comfort. They see the conversion and salvation of someone else's child and hope and pray it will happen to their child. And they wonder why it hasn't happened. The sorrow can be like that of parents who lose a child or grandchild to physical death.

"I don't know what else I can do," a distraught mother said to me. But the truth is she did know. As a believing Christian, she knew what she could do—pray and commit her wayward daughter to the Lord. What she really meant to say was "what else besides praying can I do?"

The most difficult situation for the Christian parent, grandparent, relative, or friend is overcoming the doubts, fears, and discouragement when, after years of praying, or witnessing, there is no results. The mother earlier was in such a position. Faith and prayer, she felt, had not brought results so she wondered if "works" might be necessary. This can lead to unwise words spoken to these loved ones that can in fact alienate them further away from a spiritual awakening.

There is one primary work the Christian must remain faithful in doing to reach the unconverted. That work is persistent, believing, and consistent intercessory prayer. "To him who knocks [and knocks again and again...] the door will be the opened" (Luke 11:10 NIV).

The great hope the saved always have is the ability to reach their unsaved family through the Holy Spirit. The lost are always within the realm of reachability through the prayers and faith of concern loved ones. We may not be able to speak to the lost soul, but we can always speak to God about the lost soul. As long as we are praying, we are doing something and saying s something on behalf of our loved one's spiritual awakening. Prayer is a form of witnessing. It is tapping into the power of the Holy Spirit whose work it is to "prove to the world that they are wrong about sin" (see John 16:8 TEV).

3. Live in the Present Tense
By Living in the Presence of God.

God does not want us to be so overburdened regarding any unanswered prayer petition that we are robbed of the joy of the Lord. That's why the Scripture says, "The joy of the Lord" is our strength. It is the ability to put life in perspective and trust the Lord in all our cares of life knowing He has everything under control. We honor God by accepting that He has given everyone a choice; yes, even the choice of accepting him or not. Would any of us ever try to force someone to love us. Such a thing is not love. My mother prayed for my sister Juanita and brother Jerry by saying, "whatever it takes Lord draw my daughter and son back to you." For Juanita it was cancer, for Jerry it was hitting rock bottom.

All the grandmothers I have known with a Prodigal grandson or granddaughter who came back to Father God, came by of their addiction driving them to find freedom and salvation from the Lord. God did not turn them into addicts, but their choices caused them to hit rock bottom. And as we say, "Christ is the Rock at the bottom by which those at the bottom can begin to build a new life."

In Psalms 107:26-29, the Psalmist writes: "They mount up to the heavens, they go down again to the depths; their soul melts because of trouble. They reel to and fro, and stagger like a drunken man, and are at their wit's end. Then they cry out to the Lord in their trouble, and He brings them out of their trouble." (Italics used for emphasis).

Further Bible Promises To Grandparents

Isaiah 65:23 says, They will not work in vain, and their children will not be doomed to misfortune. For they are people blessed by the Lord, and their children, too, will be blessed (NLT).

Psalm 78:6 (NLT) So each generation shall set its hope anew in God, not forgetting his glorious miracles and obey his commands.

Psalm 128:6 (NLT) May you live to enjoy your grandchildren [serving the Lord].

Isaiah 59: 21 (NLT) And this is my covenant with them, says the Lord. My Spirit will not leave them, and neither will these words I have given you. They will be on your lips and on the lips of your children and your children's children forever, I, the Lord, have spoken.

Psalm 103:17 (NLT) But the love of the Lord remains forever with those who fear him. His salvation extends to the children's children.

Psalm 102:28 (NLT) The children of your people will live in security. Their children's children will thrive in your presence.

11

The Lamp Lighters

For Zion's sake I will not hold my peace, and for Jerusalem's sake I will not rest, until his righteousness goes forth as brightness, and her salvation as a lamp that burns (Isaiah 62:1).

There are a group of men and women I want to introduce you to. They are the staff and students at the original faith-based, Bible-based, and Christ-center residential rehab program at Brooklyn Teen Challenge. This is the original flagship Center established in the early 1960's by my brother David and myself. Over the years hundreds of men and women addicted to drugs and alcohol have found a new life in Christ at this Center/Home. And it has been going now for over 65 years!

Central to the cure from life-controlling problems is prayer. These youth and adults experience the power of God as the result of the power of prayer. Chapel for them is a time of praise, worship, hearing the Word of God preached and taught—and prayer. These are weekly times of biblical Holy Spirit therapy, changing the residents to believers in Christ where the old is gone and the new is come. During chapel and other designated times of weekly staff prayer, these men and women become Lamp Lighters by praying for others. They want to be your Prayer Partner to lift up your loved one or one's before the Throne of God.

Send us their names (first names only) and these names will be written on Prayer Cards and given out to the staff and students. I personally guarantee you that your loved one will be prayed for. You can use mail or email.

Mail: Brooklyn Adult and Teen Challenge

416 Clinton Avenue, Brooklyn NY 11238

Email: prayer@bkatc.org

Doing this gives the students and staff and volunteers a way of giving back to the community of faith by being a Lamp Lighter. Here is a wonderful promise for all Lamp Lighters and those that pray for someone to have a spiritual awakening:

The people who walked in darkness, have seen a great light; those who dwelt in the land of the shadow of death, upon them a light has shined (Isaiah 9:2).

In keeping with the theme and title of this book, the "Lamp Lighters" are those who keep the light of faith, love, and truth alive in their hearts for the spiritual awakening of a loved one. Keeping this light on is one of the great challenges families have in eventually seeing a loved one become a disciple of Jesus. Lest that light goes out, it is important that the one's praying invite the oil of the Holy Spirit to continue to burn in our hearts.

I began this book with a word picture of the father of the prodigal son sitting after a day's labor on his front porch with the light from as lamp burning stay lit when he retires. The flame keeps the light burning through the darkness of the night. This is use as a metaphor for keeping the light on the heart through prayer for the homecoming of a loved one.

There are Lamp Lighters in both American history and Old Testament history who were used to light physical darkness. The spiritual Lamp Lighters are fathers and mothers, grandparents, uncles and aunts, sisters and brothers. Lamp Lighters pray that the Light of Christ penetrate the darkness of a loved one's soul so they can experience a spiritual awakening in whatever is the spiritual condition (or the lack thereof) of a loved one. Let's believe God together for the spiritual awakening of our loved ones, in Jesus' Name!

About the Author

Donald W. Wilkerson is the 5th child of Kenneth and Ann Wilkerson. He was born in Cambria County Pennsylvania into an Assembly of God pastor's home. Don, the name he goes by, was given the middle name Wesley after Charles Wesley. With that name Don contends he was destined to become a preacher! The Wilkerson family lived in North Cambria (originally Barnesboro), then moved to the Pittsburgh area for 10 years where Don in addition to being called to the ministry, also became a Pittsburg Pirate and Steeler fan. In the mid 1950's they moved to Scranton to a church where Don at the age of 16 first began to preach. From there he went to Eastern Bible Institute in Pennsylvania. There he met Cynthia Hudson from Plainfield, Vermont and they got married in 1961.

Don had already at that point been asked by his brother David to join him in New York City to work in a new street outreach to gangs called Teen Challenge. Don and Cindy moved into the first residential discipleship-rehab home at 416 Clinton Avenue Brooklyn where from then until now thousands of gang members and drug addicts have found new life in a program founded on 2 Corinthians 5:17: "If any man be in Christ Jesus; old things pass away; behold, all things become new."

Don is noted for developing the first faith-based, Christ-centered program at what has become the Flagship Center now spread around the world. In the mid 1980's Don joined his brother in founding Times Square Church where for abut 9 years Don was one of the preaching pastors. In 1995 Don then founded Global Teen Challenge, travelling the world helping to open Teen Challenge Centers in numerous countries. Don and Cindy retired to their home in Central Virginia in 2007 where he began a new ministry writing books and materials to faith-based leaders and discipleship material for students in the program. Don and Cindy interrupted retirement for a period to return to the Brooklyn Center for a more than expected long season in 2008 and then re-retied to go back to writing. Don and Cindy have 3 adult children and 5 grandchildren.

Recommended Reading List

- *Promises For Prodigals* by Lori Wilkerson Stewart
- *Prodigals & Those Who Love* Them by Ruth Bell Graham
- *How To Pray For Lost Loved* Ones by Dutch Sheets
- *Praying the Scriptures for Your Adult Children,* by Jodie Berdnt
- *The Power of Praying For Your Adult Children by* Stormie Omartian
- *Bring Your Loved Ones To Christ by* Don Wilkerson

Also By Don Wilkerson

It is said that addiction is a disease. I don't buy it, although millions do! It is to those I write. Perhaps it can be said that addiction is a choice that leads to a disease. Nevertheless, whether it is a disease or not, to me is a mute question. Addiction can be gone-gone forever, healed forever in the name and power of Jesus Christ. Let me repeat it: Addiction can be gone forever in Jesus' name! This is why I write that G.O.N.E. stands for **God Offers New Evidence** for the cure for addiction. This book is based on the Bible and its many promises.

Also by Don Wilkerson on Amazon.com

- *29:11 The Jeremiah Code: God's Incredible "Success" Plan For Your Life*
- *A Drink Called Joy, The Supernatural Answer to Addiction*
- *About Prayer!: A Beginner's Guide*
- *Bring Your Loved Ones To Christ*
- *Dear Graduate: Letters of Practical Advice*
- *Keeping the Cross Central: The Faith-Based Legacy of Teen Challenge*
- *Kept From Falling: Seven Things That Will Keep You from Falling*
- *Ministry Worker's Handbook: Twenty-Five Lessons for Rehab/Recovery Workers & Leaders*
- *The Cross Is Still Mightier Than the Switchblade*
- *The Impact of Ordinary People: Lessons from the Lesser-Known Men of the Bible*
- *The Impact of Ordinary Women in the Bible: 30 Devotional Lessons from the Lesser-Known Women of the Bible*
- *Twelve Steps Through The Bible: God's Way of Recovery From Addiction for People of Faith*
- *Your First Step to Freedom: Beginning the Journey to Finding Freedom from a Life-Controlling Problem*

Endnotes

[1] Murray, Andrew. *How to Raise Children for Christ (Updated and Annotated): A Guide for Excellent Christian Parenting*. Aneko Press. Kindle Edition.

[2] Nelson, Thomas (2013). *KJV Study Bible: Second Edition*. Thomas Nelson. Kindle Edition.

[3] Stewart, Lori Wilkerson. *Promises for Prodigals: One Hundred Biblical Promises to Declare Over Your Prodigal Guy.* Independently Published, 2018.

[4] Graham, Ruth Bell (2008*). Prodigals and Those Who Love Them: Words of Encouragement for Those Who Wait.* Baker Publishing Group. Kindle Edition.

[5] Muggeridge, Malcolm (2010). *Time and Eternity: Uncollected Writings*. Darton, Longman & Todd LTD. Kindle Edition.

[6] Graham, Ruth Bell (2008*). Prodigals and Those Who Love Them: Words of Encouragement for Those Who Wait.* Baker Publishing Group. Kindle Edition.

[7] Author Unknown.

[8] Spurgeon, Charles (2024). *Spurgeon's Sermons - Vol. XIX: The Metropolitan Tabernacle Pulpit: Spurgeon's Complete Sermons Book 19*. Kindle Edition.

[9] Linehan PhD, Marsha M. (2020). *Building a Life Worth Living: A Memoir*. Random House Publishing Group. Kindle Edition.

Feel free to contact Brother Don at…
dwilker@aol.com

Feel free to send your prayer requests to…
prayer@bkatc.org

Made in United States
Cleveland, OH
20 April 2025

16224488R00046